ARRANGED BY S T E

MW01234717

CREATED FOR THIS

TEN SONGS from TODAY'S CONTEMPORARY
CHRISTIAN ARTISTS
FOR **YOUTH CHOIR**

COMPANION PRODUCTS AVAILABLE:

Listening CD 0-7673-9943-9

Listening Cassette 0-7673-9938-2

Accompaniment CD 0-7673-9944-7 (Split-track only)

Accompaniment Cassette 0-7673-9951-X (Side A Split-track; Side B Instruments only)

CD Promo Pak 0-7673-9969-2

Cassette Promo Pak 0-7673-9973-0

Code 0-7673-9904-8

GENEVOX

FOREWORD

For approximately 10 weeks of every summer, the Centrifuge/Crosspoint section of LifeWay Christian Resources (formerly known as the Sunday School Board of the Southern Baptist Convention) touches over 54,000 students through youth camps held at over 30 locations around the world.

At Centrifuge, it is our hearts' desire to bring students to a place where they can meet God. In meeting Him, life-change takes place. Music is an important part of bringing students to the presence of their Creator. Music reaches beyond our minds and into our hearts.

I am delighted to assist Steven V. Taylor and GENEVOX MUSIC GROUP in bringing you this collection of songs for students. The wide range of musical styles will meet the needs of all your teens, as well as the adults who hear them.

So listen with your ears and, more importantly, hear with your heart.

Lance Howerton,
Centrifuge Coordinator,
LifeWay Christian Resources of the Southern Baptist Convention

Every year hundreds of students from church choirs across the U.S. converge for SonPower, a youth conference and music event at one of the nations' leading recreational and family entertainment centers. Presented by the Music Ministries Department of LifeWay Christian Resources of the Southern Baptist Convention, SonPower is five fun-filled days of Bible Study, fellowship, rehearsals, concerts, and more.

The week features appearances by Contemporary Christian artists, Bible studies led by one of the country's premiere youth speakers, and free time to enjoy the area's attractions. Highlighting the week is a once-in-a-lifetime opportunity to join together to record a music project directed by a leading producer of music for youth.

"Created for This" was recently recorded at a SonPower session under the direction of arranger Steven V. Taylor

For more information on this great event call 1-800-254-2022 or fax to 615-251-3730.

Throughout this collection, cue notes are provided when voice parts extend beyond what is often considered the natural range of the adolescent voice. Directors are encouraged to make prudent choices when assigning those notes.

CONTENTS

LifeWay staffers Greg Skipper & Robert Wagoner
flanking artist Al Denson.

I WAS CREATED FOR THIS

WORDS AND MUSIC BY LOWELL ALEXANDER AND STEVEN V. TAYLOR
ARRANGED BY STEVEN V. TAYLOR

Moving ahead (♩ = ca. 108)

SOLO *mp*

There was a ques-tion I kept ask-ing my-self; a door to be o-pened, a hope to be held. _

27

To praise the Lord with each and ev - e - ry breath, _____

Hal - le - lu - jah. _____

Dm7   G/B   Gm7   F

29

to give Him glo - ry for the God that He is. _____

Hal - le, _____ hal - le - lu - jah. __

Em7   A7/C#   Am7   G

I know — I was cre - at-ed for this. —

Hal - le, — hal - le - lu - jah. —

I know — I was cre - at-ed for this. —

Hal - le. —

48

to give Him glo - ry for the God that He is. ___

Hal - le, ___ hal - le - lu - jah. ___

F#m   B7/D#   Bm7   A

50 ⑤

Second time to Coda ⊕

I know _ I was cre - at-ed for this. _

Second time to Coda ⊕

Hal - le, ___ hal - le - lu - jah. _

Don't you know that

Second time to Coda ⊕

F#m   B7/D#   Bm9   A   A

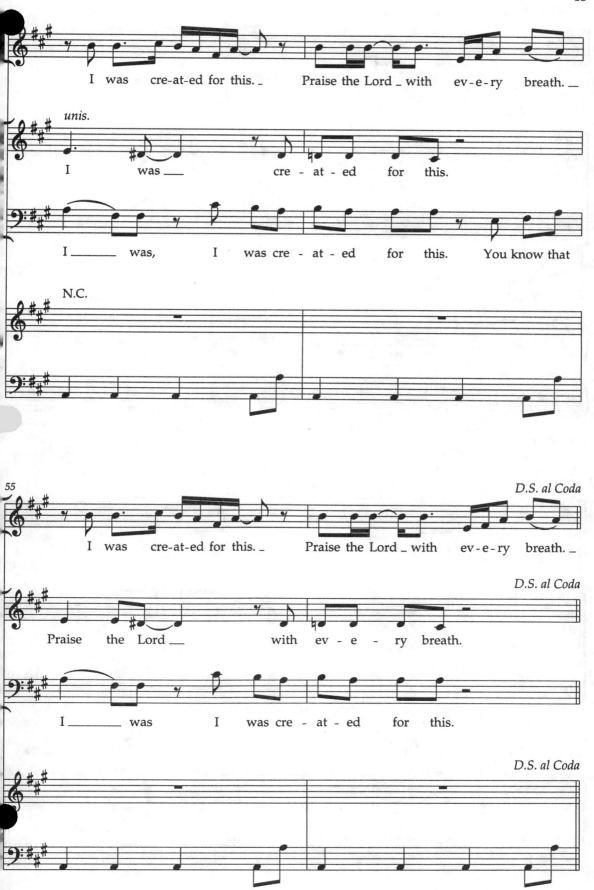

Al Denson signs autographs after concert.

SHOW YOUR POWER

WORDS AND MUSIC BY KEVIN PROSCH
ARRANGED BY STEVEN V. TAYLOR

Gently (♩ = ca. 104)

He is the Lord and

64

D.S. al Coda

div.

give us the loss.   You _____ are the Lord.   Send Your

B♭   E♭   C   *D.S. al Coda*

67 ⊕ CODA

God.   Oh Lord, our   God.   Oh Lord, our

⊕ CODA

C   F   B♭   C

70

God.   Oh Lord, our   God.

F   B♭   C   F

*Accompaniment track cuts off on beat 9.

Al Densons guitarist takes a lead.

I PROMISE

WORDS AND MUSIC BY JACI VELASQUEZ AND JOHN RAMIREZ
ARRANGED BY STEVEN V. TAYLOR

Gently (♩ = ca. 92)

Lord, You know my heart, — and all my de - sires, _

and the se - cret things _ I'll _

_____ nev-er tell; _____ Lord, You know _____ them well. _____

Though I may be young, _____ I see and un-der-stand

that at times like sheep _____ we _____

30

IF YOU LET ME LOVE YOU

WORDS AND MUSIC BY DANNY STEPHENS, MICHAEL JOHNSTON, AND MIGUEL DEJESUS
ARRANGED BY STEVEN V. TAYLOR

CHOIR

If you let _ me close, _ clos-er than _ a broth-

er. If you let _ me love _ you, we'll _ sit here _

_ and cry. _ If _ you let _ me love, _

It al - ways is giv - ing,
of - ten be - yond words. _ And when _ there's noth -
ing left _ to say, _ love has a voice.

YOU ARE HOLY AND TRUE

WORDS AND MUSIC BY LOWELL ALEXANDER AND STEVEN V. TAYLOR
ARRANGED BY STEVEN V. TAYLOR

Both times - CHOIR

ev - 'ry-thing that's _ life. _   You are peace   in all the _ noise, _

G/D   G/D   A/D

You are vi - sion in the   night. _

A/D   G   Asus

You are _ ho - ly _ and _ true, _   You are

A   D   D

23 second time

JUST AS I AM

MUSIC BY STEVEN V. TAYLOR
ARRANGED BY STEVEN V. TAYLOR

1. Just as ___ I am, ___
2. Just as ___ I am, ___

Girls sing bottom note first time through (unison Choir).

48

O God, _ I come! _ Six, sev'n, eight!

_ I come, _ I come. _

O Lamb of God, O God, I come! _

O Lamb of God,

ME WITHOUT YOU

WORDS AND MUSIC BY MARTIN BRILEY
ARRANGED BY STEVEN V. TAYLOR

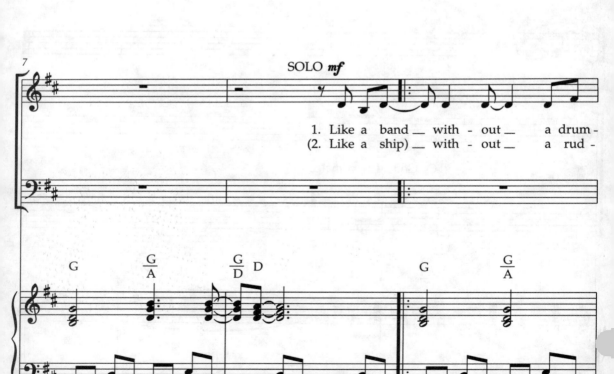

Lyrics:

1. Like a band __ with - out __ a drum __

(2. Like a ship) __ with - out __ a rud -

68

REALITY/ BREATHE ON ME

ARRANGED BY STEVEN V. TAYLOR

First time - GIRLS
Second time - CHOIR

al - i - ty that comes from a - bove, ___ God is call -

*"Reality," Words and music by STEVEN V. TAYLOR and PETER FURLER.
© 1996 Dawn Treader Music/SESAC (admin. by EMI Christian Music Group)/Warner Sojourner
Publishing/BMI. All rights reserved. Used by permission.

Steven coaches SonPower singer.

MY UTMOST FOR HIS HIGHEST

WORDS AND MUSIC BY TWILA PARIS
ARRANGED BY STEVEN V. TAYLOR

With quiet strength (♩ = ca. 66)

46

mp

GIRLS *mp*

When the Sav - ior came ___ to earth, ___

GUYS *mp*

an-swer to the end - less fall, ___

the life we live, the song we sing. For His

give my ut-most for His high - est.

An-y dream _ that tries _ to turn _ my _ heart will be _ de - nied. _